Christian Training
of Children

Christian Training of Children

A Book for Parents and Teachers

By

Charles Spurgeon

Bottom of the Hill Publishing

Memphis, TN

www.BottomoftheHillPublishing.com

ISBN: 978-1-61203-641-0

Charles Spurgeon

"Come, you children, hearken unto me—I will teach you the fear of the Lord." —Psalm 34:11

Charles Spurgeon

Content

Charles Spurgeon

FEED MY LAMBS

The best of the church are none too good for this work. Do not think because you have other service to do that therefore you should take no interest in this form of holy work, but kindly, according to your opportunities, stand ready to help the little ones, and to cheer those whose chief calling is to attend to them. To us all this message comes: "Feed My lambs!" To the minister, and to all who have any knowledge of the things of God, the commission is given. See to it that you look after the children that are in Christ Jesus. *Peter* was a leader among believers, yet he must feed the lambs.

The *lambs* are the young of the flock. So, then, we ought to look specially and carefully after those who are *young in grace*. They may be old in years, and yet they may be, mere babes in grace as

11

to the *length of their spiritual life*, and therefore they need to be under a good shepherd.

As soon as a person is converted and added to the church, he should become the object of the special care and kindness of his fellow-members. He has but newly come among us, and has no familiar friends among the saints, therefore let us all be friendly to him. Even should we leave our older comrades, we must be doubly kind towards those who are newly escaped from the world, and have come to find a refuge with the Almighty and His people. Watch with ceaseless care over those new-born babes who are strong in desires, but strong in nothing else. They have but just crept out of darkness, and their eyes can scarcely bear the light; let us be a shade to them until they grow accustomed to the blaze of gospel day.

Addict yourselves to the holy work of caring for the feeble and despondent. Peter himself that morning must have felt like a newly-enlisted soldier, for he had in a sense ended his public Christian life by denying his Lord, and he had begun it again when he "went out and wept bitterly." He was now making a new confession of his faith before his Lord and his brethren, and, therefore, because he was thus made to sympathize with recruits, he is commissioned to act as a guardian to them. Young converts are too timid to ask our help, and so our Lord introduces them to us, and with an emphatic word of command He says, "Feed My lambs!" This shall be our reward: "Inasmuch as you have done it unto one of the least of these—you have done it unto Me!"

However young a believer may be, he should make an *open confession* of his faith, and be folded with the rest of the flock of Christ. We are not among those who are suspicious of *youthful piety*: we could never see more reason for such suspicions in the case of the young, than in the case of those who repent late in life. Of the two we think the latter are more to be questioned than the former: for a selfish *fear of punishment* and dread of death are more likely to produce a *counterfeit faith* than mere childishness would be. How much has the child missed—which might have spoiled it! How much it does not know— which we hope it never may know! Oh, how much there is of brightness and trustfulness about children when converted to God which is not seen in elder converts! Our Lord Jesus evidently felt deep sympathy with children—and he is but little like Christ who looks upon them as a trouble, and treats them as if they must needs be either little deceivers or foolish simpletons. To you who teach in our schools is given this joyous privilege of finding out where these young disciples are, who are truly the lambs of Christ's flock, and to you He says, "Feed My lambs!"; that is, instruct such as are truly gracious, but young in years.

It is very remarkable that the word used here for "feed My *lambs*" is very different from the word employed in the precept, "feed My *sheep*." I will not trouble you with Greek words, but the second "feed" means exercise the office of a shepherd, rule, regulate, lead, manage them, do all that a shepherd has to do towards a flock; but this first feed does not include all that: it means distinctly *feed*, and it directs teachers to a duty which they may perhaps, neglect—namely, that of **instructing** children in the faith.

The lambs do not so much need keeping in order, as we do who know so much, and yet know so little: who think we are so far advanced that we judge one another, and contend and strive. Christian children mainly need to be taught the *doctrine*, *precept*, and *Christian living*: they require to have Divine truth put before them clearly and forcibly. Why should the higher doctrines, the *doctrines of grace*, be kept back from them? They are not as some say, *bones*; or if they are bones—they are full of marrow, and covered with fatness! If there is any doctrine too difficult for a child, it is rather the fault of the teacher's conveyance of it—than of the child's power to receive it, provided that child is really converted to God. It is ours to make doctrine simple; this is to be a main part of our work. Teach the little ones the whole truth and nothing but the truth; for instruction is the great need of the child's nature.

A child has not only to *live* as you and I have—but also to *grow*; hence he has double need of food. When fathers say of their boys, "What appetites they have!" they should remember that we also would have great appetites if we had not only to keep the machinery going, but to *enlarge* it at the same time. Children in grace have to grow, rising to greater capacity in knowing, being, doing, and feeling, and to greater power from God; therefore above all things they must be FED. They must be WELL fed or instructed, because they are in danger of having their cravings perversely satisfied with error! Youth are susceptible to false doctrine.

Whether *we* teach young Christians truth or not, the *devil* will be sure to teach them error. They will hear of it somehow, even if they are watched by the most careful guardians. The only way to keep *chaff* out of the child's little measure—is to fill it brimful with good *wheat*. Oh, that the Spirit of God may help us to do this! The more the young are taught the better; it will keep them from being misled.

We are specially exhorted to feed them—because they are so likely to be **overlooked**. I am afraid our sermons often go over the heads of the younger folk—who, nevertheless, may be as true Christians as the older ones! Blessed is he who can so speak as to be understood by a child! Blessed is that godly woman who in her class so adapts herself to girlish modes of thought—that the truth from her heart streams into the children's hearts without hindrance!

We are specially exhorted to feed the young—because this work is so **profitable**. Do what we may with people converted *late* in life—we can never make much of them. We are very glad for them for their own sakes; but at *seventy* years old—how much good can they do—even if they live another ten years? Train up a child, and he may have fifty years of holy service before him! We are glad to welcome those who come into the vineyard at the *eleventh* hour, but they have hardly taken their pruning-hook and their spade before the sun goes down, and their short day's work is ended! The time spent in training the late convert is greater than the space reserved for his actual service. But take a child-convert and teach him well, and as *early* piety often becomes *eminent* piety, and that eminent piety may have a stretch of years before it in which God may be glorified and others may be blessed, such work is profitable in a high degree.

It is also most **beneficial** work to ourselves. It exercises our *humility* and helps to keep us lowly and meek. It also trains our *patience*—let those who doubt this, try it! For even young Christians exercise the patience of those who teach them. If you want big-souled, large-hearted Christian men or women—look for them among those who are much engaged among the young, bearing with their follies, and sympathizing with their weaknesses for Jesus' sake!

DO NOT HINDER THE CHILDREN

Concerning this *hindering of children*, let us see how this is done. I think the results of this negative feeling about children coming to the Savior is to be seen, first, in the fact that often there is nothing in the service for the children. The sermon is over their heads, and the preacher does not think that this is any of his fault; in fact, he rather rejoices that it is so. Some time ago a person who wanted, I suppose, to make me feel my own insignificance, wrote to say that he had met with a number of poor people who had read my sermons with evident pleasure; and he wrote that he believed they were very suitable for poor people.

Yes, my preaching was just the sort of stuff for poor people. The gentleman did not dream what sincere pleasure he caused me; for if I am understood by poor people, by servant-girls, by children— I am sure I can be understood by others. I am ambitious of preaching for poor people—if by these you mean the lowest, the rag-tag. I think nothing greater than to win the hearts of the lowly. Just so with regard to children. People occasionally say of such a one, "He is only fit to teach children—he is no preacher." I tell you, in God's sight he is no preacher who does *not* care for the children. There should be at least a part of every sermon and service, that will suit the little ones. It is an error for us to forget this.

Parents sin in the same way when they omit true religion from the education of their children. Perhaps the thought is that their children cannot be converted while they are children, and so they think it of small consequence where they go to school in their tender years. But it is not so! Many parents even forget this when their girls and boys are ending their school-days. They send them away to colleges which are foul with every moral and spiritual danger, with the idea that there they can complete their *higher* education. In how many cases I have seen that education completed, and it has produced young *men* who are thorough-going profligates, and young *women* who are no better! As we sow—we reap.

Let us expect our children to know the Lord. Let us from the beginning mingle the name of Jesus with their A B C's. Let them read their first lessons from the Bible. It is a remarkable thing that there is no book from which children learn to read so quickly as from the New Testament! There is a charm about that Book which draws forth the infant mind. But let us never be guilty, as parents, of forgetting the religious training of our children; for if we do we may be guilty of the blood of their souls!

Another result is that the conversion of children is not expected in many of our churches and congregations. I mean, that they do not expect the children to be converted as children. The theory is that if we can impress youthful minds with principles which may, in *after* years, prove useful to them, we have done a great deal; but to convert children as *children*, and to regard them as being as much believers as their seniors, is regarded as absurd. To this *supposed absurdity* I cling with all my heart. I believe that the kingdom of God has many children—both on earth and in heaven.

Another ill-result, is that the conversion of children is not believed in. Certain suspicious people always show their teeth a bit when they hear of a newly-converted child—they will have a bite at him if they can! They very rightly insist upon it—that these children should be carefully examined before they are baptized land admitted into the church. But they are wrong in insisting that only in exceptional instances are they to be received. We quite agree with them as to the care to be exercised; but it should be the same in all cases—and neither more nor less in the cases of children.

How often do people expect to see in boys and girls the same *solemnity* of behavior which is seen in older people! It would be a good thing for us all if we had never left off being boys and girls—but had added to all the excellencies of a *child*—the virtues of a *man*. Surely it is not necessary to kill the *child*—to make the *saint!* It is thought by the more severe, that a converted child must become twenty years older in a minute!

A very solemn person once called me from the playground, and warned me of the impropriety of playing *bat and ball* with the boys. He said, "How can you play like others—if you are a child of God?" I answered that I was employed as a guardian, and it was part of my duty to join in the amusements of the boys. My venerable critic thought that this altered the matter very materially; but it was clearly his view that a converted boy, as such, ought never to *play!*

Do not others expect from children more perfect conduct than they themselves exhibit? If a gracious child should lose his temper, or act wrongly in some trifling thing through forgetfulness, straightway he is condemned as a *little hypocrite* by those who are long way from being perfect themselves! Jesus says, "Take heed that you despise not one of these little ones." Take heed that you say no unkind word against your *younger brethren* in Christ, your *little sisters* in the Lord. Jesus sets such great store by His dear *lambs*—that He carries them in His bosom! And I charge you who follow your Lord in all things—to show a like tenderness to the *little ones of the Divine family.*

"They brought young children to Him, that He should touch them. But His disciples rebuked those who brought them. But when Jesus saw it—He was *much* displeased!" He was not often displeased; certainly He was not often "*much* displeased," and when He was much displeased—we may be sure that the case was serious. He was displeased at these children being *pushed away* from Him— for it was so contrary to His mind about them.

The disciples did wrong to the **mothers**; they rebuked the parents for doing a motherly act—for doing, in fact, that which Jesus loved for them to do. They brought their children to Jesus out of respect to Him; they valued a blessing from His hands more than gold; they expected that the blessing of God would go with the touch of the great Prophet. They may have hoped that a touch of the hand of Jesus would make their children's lives bright and happy. Though there may have been a measure of *weakness* in the parents' thought—yet the Savior could not judge harshly of that which arose out of reverence to His person. He was therefore much displeased to think that those good women, who meant Him honor—should be roughly repulsed!

There was also wrong done to the **children**. Sweet little ones! What had they done that they should be chided for coming to Jesus? They had not meant to intrude. Dear things! they would have fallen at His feet in reverent love for the sweet-voiced Teacher, who charmed not only men—but children, by His tender Words. The little ones meant nothing bad—and why should they be blamed?

Besides, there was wrong done to **Jesus** Himself. It might have made men think that Jesus was stiff, reserved, and self-exalted, like the Rabbis. If they had thought that He could not condescend to children—they would have sadly slandered the reputation of His great love. His heart was a *great harbor* wherein many *little ships* might cast anchor. Jesus, the child-man, was never more at home than with children! The holy child Jesus had an affinity for children! Was He to be represented by His own disciples—as shutting the door against the children? This would do a sad injury to His real character!

Therefore, grieved at the triple evil which wounded the *mothers*, the *children*, and Himself—He was greatly displeased. Anything we do to hinder a dear child from coming to Jesus, greatly displeases our dear Lord. He cries to us, "Stand back! Let them alone! Let them come to Me—and forbid them not!"

Next, it was contrary to His **teaching**, for He went on to say, "I assure you: Whoever does not enter the kingdom of God like a little child, will never enter it!" Christ's teaching was not that there is *something in us* to fit us for the kingdom; and that a certain number of years may make us capable of receiving grace. His teaching all went the other ways—namely, that we are to be *nothing*, and that the *less* we are and the *weaker* we are—the better! For the less we have of *SELF*—the more room there is for His divine grace. Do you think to come to Jesus up the ladder of *knowledge*? Come down! You must meet Him at the foot. Do you think to reach Jesus up the steep hill of *experience*? Come down, dear climber; He stands in the plain!

"Oh! but when I am *old*—I shall then be prepared for Christ." Stay where you are, *young man!* Jesus meets you at the door of life; you were never more fit to meet Him than just *now*. He asks nothing of you—but that you will be nothing, and that He may be all in all to you. That is His teaching—and to send back the child because it has not *this* or *that*—is to fly in the teeth of the blessed doctrine of the grace of God.

Once more, it was quite contrary to Jesus Christ's **practice**. He made them see this; for "He took them up in His arms, put His hands upon them, and blessed them." All His life long, there is nothing in Him like rejection and refusing. He said truly, "the one who comes to Me—I will never cast out!" If He did cast out any because they were too young—the text would be falsified at once—but that can never be. He is the receiver of all who sincerely come to Him. It is written, "This Man receives sinners, and eats with them."

His life might be drawn, as a *"Shepherd*

with a lamb in His bosom!" And never as a cruel shepherd setting his dogs upon the lambs and driving them and their mothers away!

Charles Spurgeon

THE DISCIPLES AND THE MOTHERS

The immediate disciples of our Lord were a highly honorable band of men. Despite their mistakes and shortcomings, they must have been greatly *sweetened* by living near to one so perfect and so full of love. I gather, therefore, that if these men, who were the *cream of the cream*, rebuked the mothers who brought their young children to Christ— then this must be a pretty common offense in the church of God. I fear that the chilling frost of this mistake is felt almost everywhere. I am not going to make any uncharitable statements; but I think if a little personal investigation were made, that many of us might find ourselves guilty upon this point, and might be led to cry with Pharaoh's butler, *"I do remember my faults this day!"*

Have we laid ourselves out for the conversion of children—as much as we have done for the conversion of grown-up-folks? What! Do you think me sarcastic? Do you not lay yourselves out for *anybody's* conversion? What must I say to you? It is dreadful that the *Cainite* spirit should enter a believer's heart and make him say, "Am I my brother's keeper?" It is a shocking thing, that *we ourselves* should eat the fat, and drink the sweet—and leave the famishing multitudes to perish. But tell me now, if you did care for the salvation of souls, would you not think it rather too commonplace a matter to begin with boys and girls? Yes! And your feeling is shared by many. The fault is common.

I believe, however, that this feeling, in the case of the apostles, was caused by **zeal for Jesus**. These good men thought that the bringing of children to the Savior would cause an *interruption*. They thought that He was engaged in much better work—He had been confounding the Pharisees, instructing the masses, and healing the sick. Could it be right to pester Him with *children*? The little ones would not understand His teaching, and they did not need His miracles—so why should they be brought in to disturb His great doings? Therefore the disciples as good as said, "Take your children back, good women. Teach them the law yourselves, and pray with them. Every child cannot have Christ's hands laid on it. If we allow one set of children to come—then we would have all the neighborhood swarming about us—and the Savior's work will be grievously interrupted! Don't you see this? Why do you act so thoughtlessly towards Jesus?"

The disciples had such reverence for their Master—that they would send the *prattlers* away, lest the great Rabbi should seem to become a mere *teacher of babes*. This may have been a *zeal* for God—but it was not according to knowledge.

Thus in these days, certain brethren would hardly like to receive many children into the church, lest it should become a *society of boys and girls*. Surely, if these come into the church in any great numbers, the church may be spoken of in terms of reproach! The outside world will call it a mere Sunday-school!

I remember that when an immoral woman had been converted in one of our county-towns, there was an objection among certain professors to her being received into the church; and certain proud fellows even went the length of advertising in the newspapers, the fact that the Baptist minister had baptized a harlot! I told my friend to regard it as an *honor*. Just so, if any *reproach* us with receiving young children into the church, we will wear the reproach as a *badge of honor*.

Holy children cannot possibly do us any harm. God will send us sufficient people of age and experience to steer the church prudently. We will receive none who fail to yield *evidence of the new birth*, however *old* they may be! But we will shut out no believers, however *young* they may be. God forbid that we should condemn our cautious brethren—but at the same time—we wish their caution would show itself where it is more required. Jesus will not be dishonored by the *children*—we have, far more cause to fear the *adults!*

The apostles' rebuke of the children arose in measure from **ignorance of the children's need**. If any mother in that throng had said, "I must bring my child to the Master, for he is sore afflicted with a *devil*," then neither Peter, nor James, nor John, would have demurred for a moment—but would have assisted in bringing the demon possessed child to the Savior. Or suppose another mother had said, "My child has a deadly sickness upon it—it is wasted down to skin and bone; permit me to bring my darling, that Jesus may lay His hands upon her,"—the disciples would all have said: "*Make way* for this woman and her sorrowful burden."

But *these* little ones with bright eyes, and prattling tongues, and leaping limbs—why should *they* come to Jesus? They forgot that in those children, with all their joy, their health, and their apparent innocence—that there was a great and grievous need for the blessing of a Savior's grace. If you indulge in the novel idea that your children do not need conversion, that children born of Christian parents are somewhat superior to others, and have *good within them* which only needs *development*, one great motive for your devout earnestness will be gone.

Believe me, *your* children need the Spirit of God to give them new hearts and right spirits—or else they will go astray just as other children do. Remember that however young they are— that there is a stone within the youngest heart—and that stone must be taken away, or be the ruin of the child! There is a *tendency to evil* in every child—even where as yet it is not developed into act, and that tendency needs to be overcome by the divine power of the Holy Spirit, causing the child to be born again.

Oh, that the church of God would cast

off the old *Jewish* idea which still has such force around us—namely, that *natural birth* brings with it covenant privileges! Now, even under the Old Dispensation there were hints that the *true* seed was not born after the *flesh*—but after the *Spirit*, as in the case of Ishmael and Isaac, and Esau and Jacob. Does not even the *church of God* know that "That which is born of the flesh is flesh; and that which is born of the Spirit is spirit"? "Who can bring a clean thing out of an unclean thing?" The natural *birth* communicates nature's *filthiness*—but it cannot convey *grace!*

Under the *new covenant*, we are *expressly* told that the sons of God are "born *not* of blood, nor of the will of the flesh, nor of the will of man—but of God." Under the old covenant, which was typical, the birth according to the flesh yielded *privilege*; but to come at all under the covenant of grace—you must be born again. The first birth brings you nothing but an inheritance with the *first* Adam! You must be born again to come under the headship of the *second* Adam.

But it is written, says one, "that the promise is unto you, and to your *children*." There never was a grosser piece of knavery committed under heaven, than the quotation of that text as it is usually quoted. I have heard it quoted many times to prove a doctrine which is very far removed from that which it clearly teaches. If you take *one-half* of any sentence which a man utters, and leave out the rest—you may make him say the opposite of what he means. What do you think that text *really* says? See Acts 2:39, "The promise is unto you and to your children, and to all that are afar off—even *as many as the Lord our God shall call.*" This grandly wide statement is the argument on which is founded the exhortation, "Repent, and be baptized every one of you." It is not a declaration of privilege special to anyone—but a presentation of grace as much to all who are afar off—as to them and to their children. There is not a word in the New Testament to show that the benefits of divine grace are in any degree transmitted by natural descent. The benefits of divine grace come "to as many as the Lord our God shall call," whether their parents are saints—or unconverted sinners. How can people have the impudence to tear off half a text to make it teach what is not true?

You must sorrowfully look upon your child then—as "born in sin, and shaped in iniquity, and heirs of wrath, even as others!" And though you may yourself belong to a line of saints, and trace your pedigree from minister to minister, all eminent in the church of God—yet your children occupy precisely the same position by their birth—as other people's children do! They too, must be *redeemed* from under the curse of the law by the precious blood of Jesus, and they must receive a *new nature* by the work of the Holy Spirit. They are favored by being placed under godly training, and under the hearing of the gospel; but their need and their sinfulness are the same as in the rest of the human race. If you think of this, you will see the reason why they should be brought to Jesus Christ—a reason why they should be brought as speedily as possible in the *arms of your prayer and faith* to Him who alone is able to renew them.

I have sometimes met with a deeper spiritual experience in children of ten and twelve—than I have in certain people of fifty and sixty! It is an old proverb that "some children are born with beards". Some *boys* are *little men,* and some *girls* are *little old women.* You cannot measure the *lives* of any of us by our *ages.* I knew a boy who, when he was fifteen, often heard old Christian people say, "The *boy* is sixty years old—he speaks with such insight into divine truth!" I believe that this youth at fifteen, did know far more of the things of God, and of soul travail, than any around him, whatever their age might be.

I cannot tell you why it is—but so it is in fact—that some are old when they are young, and some are very green when they are old. Some are *wise* when you would expect them to be *otherwise*; and others are very foolish when you might have expected that they had grown out of their folly.

Do not talk of a child's *incapacity for repentance!* I have known a child weep herself to sleep for months, under a crushing sense of sin. If you would know a deep, and bitter, and solemn fear of the *wrath* of God, let me tell you what *I* felt as a boy. If you would know *joy* in the Lord, many a child has been as full of joy—as his little heart could hold. If you want to know what *faith* in Jesus is, you must not look to those who have been bemuddled by the heretical jargon of the times—but to the dear children who have taken Jesus at His word, and believed in Him, and loved Him—and therefore know and are sure that they are saved.

Capacity for believing lies more in the *child*—than in the *man*. We grow less rather capable of faith—than more capable of faith. Every year brings the unregenerate mind *further* away from God, and makes it less capable of receiving the things of God. No *ground* is more prepared for the good seed—than that which as yet has not been trodden down as the highway, nor has been as yet overgrown with thorns. Not yet has the child learned the deceits of pride, the falsehood of ambition, the delusions of worldliness, the tricks of trade, the sophistries of philosophy; and so far it has an *advantage* over the adult. In any case—the new birth is the work of the Holy Spirit, and He can as easily work upon youth as upon old age.

Some, too, have hindered the children because they have been *forgetful of the child's value*. The soul's price does not depend upon its years. "Oh, it is *only* a child!" "Children are a nuisance." "Children are always getting in the way." This talk is common. God forgive those who despise the little ones! Will you be very angry, if I say that a *boy* is more worth saving than a grown man? It is infinite mercy on God's part to save those who are seventy; for what good can they now do with the fag-end of their lives? When we get to be fifty or sixty, we are almost worn out; and if we have spent all our early days with the devil—then what remains for God?

But these dear boys and girls—there is something to be made out of them. If now they yield themselves to Christ, they may have a long, happy, and holy life before them, in which they may serve God with all their hearts. Who knows what glory God may have from them? Heathen hands may call them blessed. Whole nations may be enlightened by them. If a famous schoolmaster was accustomed to take his hat off to his boys, because he did not know whether one of them might not be Prime Minister, we may justly look upon converted children, for we do not know how soon they may be among the angels, or how greatly their light may shine among men. Let us estimate children at their true valuation, and we shall not keep them back—but we shall be eager to lead them to Jesus at once.

In proportion to our own spirituality of mind, and in proportion to our own child-likeness of heart, we shall be at home with children; and we shall enter into their early fears and hopes, their budding faith and opening love.

Dwelling among young converts, we shall seem to be in a garden of flowers, in a vineyard where the tender grapes give a good fragrance.

Charles Spurgeon

THE CHILDREN'S SHEPHERD

First, the **person** who is called to feed the lambs.

Simon Peter was not a Welshman—but he had a great deal of what we know as *Welsh fire* in him. He was just the sort of man to interest the young. Children delight to gather round a **fire**, whether it be on the *hearth* or in the *heart*. Certain people appear to be made of ice, and from these children speedily shrink away. Congregations or classes grow smaller every Sunday when cold-blooded creatures preside over them. But when a man or a woman has a kindly heart, the children seem to gather readily, just as flies in autumn days swarm on a warm, sunny wall. Therefore Jesus

41

says to warm-hearted Simon, "Feed My lambs!" He is the man for the office.

Simon Peter was, moreover, an **experienced** man. He had known his own weakness; he had felt the pangs of conscience; he had sinned much and had been much forgiven, and now he was brought in tender humility to confess the love and loveliness of Jesus. We want experienced men and women to talk to converted children, and to tell them what the Lord has done for them, and what have been their dangers, their sins, their sorrows, and their comforts. The young are glad to hear the story of those who have been further along the road than they have. I may say of experienced saints—their lips preserve knowledge. Experience lovingly narrated, is suitable food for young believers, instruction such as the Lord is likely to bless to their nourishing in grace.

Simon Peter was now a greatly **indebted** man. He owed much to Jesus Christ, according to that rule of the Kingdom, "he loves much—to whom much has been forgiven."

Oh, you who have never entered upon this service for Christ, and yet might do it well, come forward at once and say, "I have left this work to younger hands—but I will do so no longer. I have experience, and I trust I yet retain a warm heart within my bosom; I will go and join these workers, who are steadily feeding the lambs in the name of the Lord."

Thus far, as to the *person* who is called to feed the lambs.

When the Lord calls a man to a work, He gives him the **preparation** necessary for it. How was Peter prepared for feeding Christ's lambs?

First, by being *fed himself.* The Lord gave him a breakfast before giving him a commission. You cannot feed lambs, or sheep either—unless you are first fed yourself. It is quite right for you to be teaching a great part of the Lord's day; but I think a teacher is very unwise who does not *first* come to hear the gospel preached and get a meal for his own soul. First be fed—and then feed.

But especially Peter was prepared for feeding the lambs, by *being with his Master.* He would never forget that morning, and all the incidents of it. It was Christ's *voice* that he heard; it was Christ's *look* that pierced him to the heart. He breathed the air which surrounded the risen Lord, and this fellowship with Jesus perfumed Peter's heart and tuned Peter's speech, that he might afterwards go forth and feed the lambs.

I commend to you the study of *instructive books*—but above all I commend the study of *Christ Himself.* Let *Him* be your library. Get near to Jesus. An hour's communion with Jesus—is the best preparation for teaching either the young or the old.

Peter was also prepared in a more painful way than that—namely, by *self-examination*. The question came to him thrice over, "Simon, son of Jonah, Do you love Me? Do you love Me? Do you love Me?" Often the vessel needs scouring with self-examination, before the Lord can fitly use it to convey the living water to thirsting ones. It never hurts a true-hearted man to search his own spirit, and to be searched and tried by his Lord. It is the hypocrite who is afraid of the truth which tests his profession: trying discourses, and trying meditations—he dreads. But the genuine man wants to know for certain, that he really does love Christ, and therefore he looks within him—and questions and cross-questions himself.

Mainly that examination should be exercised concerning our **love**; for the best preparation for teaching Christ's lambs is love—love to Jesus and to them. We cannot be priests on their behalf, unless like Aaron we wear their names upon our breasts. We must love—or we cannot bless. Teaching is poor work—when love is gone; it is like a black-smith working without fire, or a builder without mortar. A shepherd who does not love his sheep—is a hireling and not a shepherd. He will flee in the time of danger, and leave his flock to the wolf. Where there is no love—there will be no life; *living lambs* are not to be fed by *dead men*. We preach and teach love—our *subject* is the love of God in Christ Jesus. How can we teach this—if we have no love ourselves? Our *object* is to create love in the hearts of those we teach, and to foster it where it already exists; but how can we convey the *fire* if it is not kindled in our own hearts? How can he promote the *flame* whose hands are damp, and dripping with worldliness and indifference, so that he acts on the child's heart rather as a *bucket of water*—than as a *flame of fire?*

These lambs of the flock live in the love of Christ—shall they not live in our love? He calls them His lambs, and so they are; shall we not love them for His sake? They were *chosen* in love; they were *redeemed* in love; they have been *called* in love; they have been *washed* in love; they have been *fed* by love, and they will be *kept* by love until they come to the green pastures on the hilltops of heaven. You and I will be out of gear with the vast machinery of divine love—unless our souls are full of affectionate zeal for the good of the beloved ones. Love is the

45

grandest preparation for the ministry, whether exercised in the *congregation*, or in the *class*. Love—and then feed. If you love—feed. If you do not love—then wait until the Lord has quickened you, and lay not your unhallowed hand to this sacred service!

With the weak of the flock, with the new converts in the flock, with the young children in the flock—our principal **business** is to **FEED**. Every sermon, every lesson, should be a feeding sermon and a feeding lesson. It is of little use to stand and thump the Bible and call out, "Believe, believe, believe!" when nobody knows what is to be believed. I see no use in fiddles and tambourines; neither lambs nor sheep can be fed upon *brass bands*. There must be doctrine—solid, sound, gospel doctrine to constitute real feeding.

When you have a joint of meat on the table—then ring the dinner-bell; but the bell alone, feeds nobody if no food is served up. Getting children to meet in the morning and the afternoon is a waste of both their steps and yours—if you do not set before them soul-saving, soul-sustaining truth! Feed the lambs; you need not play music to them, nor put garlands round their necks; nor entertain them in any way—but do *feed* them!

This feeding is humble, lowly, **unostentatious** work. Do you know the name of any shepherd? I have known the names of one or two shepherds—but I never heard anybody speak of them as *great* men. Their names are not in the papers, nor are they before the public eye. Shepherds are generally quiet, unobtrusive people. When you look at the shepherd, you would not see any difference between him and the ploughman. The shepherd plods on uncomplainingly through the winter, and in the early spring he has no rest night or day because the lambs are needing him. This he does year after year, and yet he will never be made a Knight, nor even be exalted to a Noble, albeit he may have done far more useful work than those who are floated into fame. Just so in the case of many a faithful teacher of young children; you hear but little about him—yet he is doing grand work for which future ages will call him blessed. His Master knows all about him, and we shall hear of him in *that great and final* day; but perhaps not until then.

Feeding the lambs is **careful** work, too—for lambs cannot be fed on anything you please, especially Christ's lambs. You can soon *half-poison* young believers with bad teaching. Christ's lambs are all too apt to eat herbs which are injurious—we need to be cautious where we lead them. If men are to take heed what they *hear*—how much more should we take heed what we *teach*. It is careful work—the feeding of each lamb separately, and the teaching of each child by itself the truth which it is best able to receive.

Moreover, this is **continuous** work. "Feed My lambs," is not for a season—but for all time. Lambs could not live if the shepherd only fed them once a week. They would die between Sundays; therefore good teachers of the young look after them all the days of the week as they have opportunity, and they are careful to feed their souls with *prayer* and *holy example* when they are not teaching them by word of mouth. The shepherding of lambs is daily, hourly work. When is a shepherd's work over? How many hours a day does he labor? He will tell you that in lambing-time, he is never done. He sleeps just when he is able, taking much less than forty winks, and then rousing himself for action. It is so with those who feed Christ's lambs; they rest not until God saves and sanctifies their dear ones.

It is **laborious** work, too. At the least, he who does not labor at it will have a terrible account to render. Do you think a minister's life is an easy one? I tell you that he who makes it so—will find it hard enough when he comes to the day of judgment! Nothing so exhausts a man who is called to it—as the care of souls. Just so it is in measure, with all who teach—they cannot do good without spending themselves.

You must study the lesson; you must bring forth something fresh to your class; you must instruct and impress. I have no doubt you are often driven very hard for matter, and wonder how you will get through the next Lord's-day. I know you are sorely pressed at times, if you are worth your salt. You dare not rush to your class unprepared, and offer to the Lord that which costs you nothing. There must be labor—if the food is to be *wisely* placed before the lambs, so that they can receive it.

And all this has to be done in a singularly choice spirit; the true shepherd spirit is an amalgam of many precious graces. He is hot with zeal—but he is not fiery with passion; he is gentle—and yet he rules his class; he is loving—but he does not wink at sin; he has power over the lambs—but he is not domineering or sharp; he has cheerfulness—but not levity; he has freedom—but not license; he has solemnity—but not gloom. He who cares for lambs—should be a lamb himself! And blessed be God, there is a Lamb before the throne who cares for all of us, and does so the more effectually, because He is in all things made like unto us.

The shepherd spirit is a *rare* and *priceless* gift! A successful pastor or a successful teacher in a school will be found to have special characteristics, which distinguish him from his fellows. A bird when it is sitting on its eggs, or when the little ones are newly-hatched, has about it a *mother-spirit*, so that it devotes all its life to the feeding of its little ones. Other birds may be taking their pleasure on the wing—but this bird sits still the long day and night, or else its only flights are to provide for gaping mouths which seem to be never filled. A passion has taken possession of the bird; and something like it comes over the true soul-winner: he would gladly die to win souls! He pines, he pleads, he plods to bless those on whom his heart is set. He would pawn half his heaven—if these souls could but be saved! And sometimes, in moments of enthusiasm he is ready to barter heaven altogether to win souls; and, like Paul, he could wish himself accursed, so that they were but saved. This blessed zeal, many cannot understand, because they never felt it. May the Holy Spirit work it in us, so shall we act as true shepherds towards the lambs. This, then, is the work: "Feed My lambs!"

MODEL LESSON FOR TEACHERS

Teach them **morality**: "Keep your *tongue* from evil, and your *lips* from speaking deceit. Depart from evil, and do good; seek peace, and pursue it." Now, we never teach morality as the way of salvation. God forbid that we should ever mix up man's works in any way with the redemption which is in Christ Jesus! "By grace are you saved through faith, and that not of yourselves, it is the gift of God." Yet we teach morality while we teach spirituality; and I have always found that the gospel produces the best morality in all the world. I would have a Sunday-school teacher watchful over the morals of the boys and girls under his care, speaking to them very particularly of those sins which are most common to youth. He may honestly and conveniently say many things to his children which no one else can say, especially when reminding them of the sin of *lying*, so common with children, or the sin of *petty theft*, or of *disobedience* to parents. I would have the teacher be very particular in mentioning these evils one by one; for it is of little avail talking to them about *sins in the mass*, you must take them one by one, just as David did.

First look after the tongue: "Keep your tongue from evil, and your lips from speaking deceit." Then look after the whole conduct. "Depart from evil, and do good; seek peace, and pursue it." If the child's soul is not saved by other parts of the teaching, this part may have a beneficial effect upon his life, and so far so good. Morality, however, by itself is comparatively a small thing.

The best part of what you teach is **godliness**. I said not, "religion," but *godliness*. Many people are *religious after a fashion*, without being godly. Many have all the externals of godliness, all the outside of piety; such men we call "religious," but they have no right thought about God. They think about their place of worship, their Sunday, their books—but nothing about God. He who does not respect God, pray to God, love God—is an ungodly man, whatever his external religion may be.

Labor to teach the child always to have an eye to God; write on his memory these words, "You O God, see me!" Bid him remember that his every act and thought are under the eye of God. No Sunday-school teacher discharges his duty unless he constantly lays stress upon the fact that there is a God who notices everything that happens. Oh, that we were more godly ourselves; that we talked more of godliness, and that we loved godliness better!

The third lesson is, the evil of **sin**. If the child does not learn that, he will never learn the way to Heaven. None of us ever knew what a Savior Christ was—until we knew what an evil thing sin was. If the Holy Spirit does not teach us the exceeding sinfulness of sin, we shall never know the blessedness of salvation. Let us seek His grace, then, when we teach, that we may always be able to lay stress upon the abominable nature of sin.

"The face of the Lord is against those who do evil, to cut off the remembrance of them from the earth." Do not spare your child; let him know what sin leads to. Do not, like some people, be afraid of speaking plainly and broadly concerning the consequences of sin.

I have heard of a father, one of whose

sons, a very ungodly youth, died in a very sudden manner. The father did not, as some would have done, say to his family, "We hope your brother has gone to Heaven." No! but overcoming his natural feelings, he was enabled, by Divine grace, to assemble his children together, and to say to them, "My sons and daughters, your brother is dead—and I fear he is in hell. You knew his life and conduct, you saw how he behaved; and now God has snatched him away in his sins!" Then he solemnly told them of the place of woe, to which he believed—yes, almost knew he was gone, begging them to shun it, and to flee from the wrath to come! Thus he was the means of bringing his children to serious thought.

But had he acted, as some would have done, with tenderness of heart—but not with honesty of purpose, and said he hoped his son had gone to Heaven, what would the other children have said? "If brother has gone to Heaven—then there is no need for us to fear; we may live as we like—and still arrive in heaven."

No, no! It is not unchristian to say of some men, that they are gone to hell, when we have seen that their lives have been hellish lives. But it is asked, "Can you judge your fellow-creatures?" No— but I can know them by their *fruits*. I do not judge them, or condemn them; they judge themselves! I have seen their sins go beforehand to judgment—and I do not doubt that they shall follow after.

"But may they not be saved at the *eleventh hour?*" I have heard of *one* who was—but I do not know that there ever was another, and I cannot tell that there ever will be.

Be honest, then, with your children, and teach them, by the help of God, that "evil shall slay the wicked!"

Children need to learn their **need** of a Savior. You must not hold back from this needful task. Do not flatter the child with delusive rubbish about his nature being good. Tell him he must be born again. Don't bolster him up with the dream of his own innocence—but show him his sin. Mention the childish sins to which he is prone, and pray the Holy Spirit to work conviction in his heart and conscience. Deal with the young in much the same way as you would with the old. Be thorough and honest with them. *Flimsy religion* is neither good for young nor old. These boys and girls need pardon through the precious blood as surely as any of us. Do not hesitate to tell the child his *ruin*; he will not else desire the *remedy*. Tell him also of the *punishment* of sin, and warn him of its terror. Be tender—but be true. Do not hide from the youthful sinner the truth, however dreadful it may be. If he believes not in Christ, it will go ill with him at the last great day. Set before him the final judgment, and remind him that he will have to give an account of things done in the body. Labor to arouse the conscience; and pray God the Holy Spirit to work by you until the heart becomes tender, and the mind perceives the need of the great salvation.

But you will not have done half enough unless you teach carefully the fourth lesson—the absolute necessity of a **change of heart**. "The Lord is near unto those who are of a broken heart; and saves such as are of a contrite spirit." Oh! may God enable us to keep this constantly before the minds of those we teach—that there must be a broken heart and a contrite spirit, that good works will be of no avail unless there is a new nature, that the most arduous duties and the most earnest prayers will all be as nothing, unless there be a true and thorough repentance for sin, and an entire forsaking of sin through the grace and mercy of God!

Be sure, whatever you leave out, that you teach the children the **three R's**,— Ruin, Redemption, and Regeneration. Tell the children they are *ruined* by the Fall, and that there is salvation for them only by being *redeemed* by the blood of

Jesus Christ, and *regenerated* by the Holy Spirit. Keep constantly before them these vital truths, and then you will have the pleasing task of telling them the sweet subject of the closing lesson.

In the fifth place, tell the children of the joy and **blessedness** of being Christians. "The Lord redeems the soul of His servants: and none of those who trust in Him shall be desolate." I need not tell you how to talk about that theme; for if you know what it is to be a Christian, you will never be short of subject matter. When we get on this subject, our mind cares not to speak; it would rather revel in its bliss. Truly was it said, "Blessed is he whose transgression is forgiven, whose sin is covered." "Blessed is that man who makes the Lord his trust." Yes, truly, blessed is the man, the woman, the child who trusts in the Lord Jesus Christ, and whose hope is in Him.

Always lay a stress; upon this point— that the righteous are a blessed people, that the chosen family of God, redeemed by blood and saved by power, are a blessed people while here below, and that they will be a blessed people forever in Heaven above. Let your children see that you belong to that blessed company. If they know you are in trouble, if it is possible, come to your class with a smiling face, so that your scholars may be able to say: "Teacher is a blessed man, although he is bowed down by his troubles." Always seek to keep a joyous face, that your boys and girls may know that your religion is a blessed reality. Let this be one main point of your teaching, that though "many are the afflictions of the righteous," yet "the Lord delivers him out of them all. None of those who trust in Him shall be desolate."

Thus have I given you five lessons; and now let me solemnly say that, with all the instruction you may give to your children, you must all of you be deeply conscious that you are not capable of doing anything in the securing of the child's salvation—but that it is God Himself who, from the first to the last, must effect it all. You are simply a *pen*; God can write with you—but you cannot write anything of yourself. You are a *sword*; God can slay the child's sin with you—but you cannot slay it of yourself. Be, therefore, always mindful of this, that you must be first taught of God yourself—and then you must ask God to use you to teach; for unless a higher Teacher than you works and instructs the child—the child must perish. It is not your instruction which can save the souls of your children; it is the blessing of God the Holy Spirit accompanying your labors! May God bless and crown your efforts with abundant success! He will surely do so if you are instant in prayer, constant in supplication. Never yet did the earnest teacher or preacher "labor in vain in the Lord," and often has it been seen that bread cast upon the waters has been found after many days.

Charles Spurgeon

COME, YOU CHILDREN

"Come, you children, hearken unto me—I will teach you the fear of the Lord." Psalm 34:11

Three admonitions

First, recollect **whom** you are teaching: "Come, you *children*." I think we ought always to have respect to our audience; I do not mean that we need care if we are preaching to *Mr. So-and-so, Sir William* this, or *My Lord* that—because in God's sight such titles are the merest trifles; but we are to remember that we are preaching to men and women who have souls, so that we ought not to occupy their time by things that are not worth their hearing. But when you teach in Sunday-schools, you are, if it be possible, in a more responsible situation even than a minister occupies. He preaches to grown-up people, to men of judgment, who, if they do not like what he preaches, can go somewhere else; but you teach children who have no option of going elsewhere. If you teach the child wrongly—he believes you; if you teach him heresies—he will receive them; what you teach him now—he will never forget. You are not sowing, as some say, on virgin soil, for it has long been occupied by the devil; but you are sowing on a soil more fertile now than it ever will be again—soil that will produce fruit now, far better than it will do in after days; you are sowing on a young heart, and what you sow will be pretty sure to abide there, especially it you teach evil, for that will never be forgotten.

You are beginning with the child; take care what you do with him. Do not spoil him. Many a child has been treated like the Indian children who have heavy copper plates put upon their heads—so that they may never grow. There are many who are simpletons as adults, just because those who had the care of them when young, gave them no opportunities of getting knowledge, so that, when they became old, they cared nothing about it. Consider what you are after—you are teaching children, mind what you teach them. Put poison in the spring, and it will pollute the whole stream. Take care what you are after! You are twisting the *sapling*, and the old oak will be bent thereby. Have a care, it is a child's soul you are tampering with! It is a child's soul you are preparing for eternity! I give you a solemn admonition on every child's behalf. Surely, if it be murder to administer poison to the dying, it must be far more criminal to give poison to the young life! If it is evil to mislead grey-headed old age, it must be far more so to turn aside the feet of the young into the road of error, in which they may walk forever!

Second, recollect that **you are teaching for God,** "Come, you children, hearken unto me—I will teach you the fear of the Lord." If you, as teachers, were only assembled to teach *geography*, it might not injure them eternally if you were to tell the children that the North Pole was close to the Equator; or if you were to say that the extremity of South America was near by the coast of Europe; or if you assured them that England was in the middle of Africa. But you are not teaching geography, or astronomy, nor are you training the children for a business life in this world; but you are, to the best of your ability, teaching them for God.

You say to them, "Children, you come here to be taught the Word of God; you come here, if it be possible, that we may be the means of the salvation of your souls." Have a care what you are after, when you attempt to be teaching them for God. Wound the child's *hand* if you will; but, for God's sake, do not wound his eternal *soul*. Say what you like about temporal things; but, I beseech you, in spiritual matters, take care how you lead them. Be careful that it is the truth which you inculcate, and only that. With such a responsibility, how solemn your work becomes! He who is doing a work for himself—may do it as he likes; but he who is laboring for another—must take care to please his master. He who is employed by a *monarch* must beware how he performs his duty; but he who labors for *God* must tremble lest he does his work badly. Remember that you are laboring for God, if you are what you profess to be. Alas! many, I fear, are far from having this *serious view* of the work of a Sunday-school teacher.

Third, remember that **your children need teaching**. "Come, you children, hearken unto me—I will teach you the fear of the Lord." That makes your work all the more solemn. If children did not need teaching, I would not be so extremely anxious that you should teach them aright. Works that are not necessary, men may do as they please; but this work is absolutely necessary. Your child needs teaching. He was born in iniquity; in sin did his mother conceive him. He has an evil heart. He knows not God, and he never will know the Lord, unless he is taught.

He is not like some ground of which we have heard, that has *good seed* lying hidden deep in the soil; but, instead thereof, he has only *evil seed* within his heart. God can place good seed there. You profess to be His instruments to scatter good seed upon that child's heart; remember, if that seed is not sown—he will be lost forever; his life will be a life of alienation from God; and at his death everlasting punishment must be his portion! Be careful, then, how you teach, remembering the urgent necessity of the case.

This is not a house on fire, needing your assistance at the pumps; nor is it a wreck at sea, demanding your help in the lifeboat; but it is an *eternal soul* calling aloud to you, "Come and help me!" Therefore, I beseech you, teach the fear of the Lord, and that only. Be very anxious to say, and to say truly, "Come, you children, hearken unto me—I will teach you the fear of the Lord." Psalm 34:11

The Psalmist's invitation

"Come, you children, hearken unto me—I will teach you the fear of the Lord."
Psalm 34:11

It is a singular thing that good men frequently discover their duty when they are placed in most humiliating positions. Never in David's life was he in a worse plight than that which suggested this Psalm. It is headed, "A Psalm of David, when he changed his behavior before Abimelech; who drove him away, and he departed." This poem was intended to commemorate that event, and was suggested by it. David was carried before King Achish, and, in order to make his escape, he pretended to be insane, accompanying that profession of madness with certain very degrading actions which might well seem to betoken his insanity. He, was driven from the palace, and as usual, when such men are in the street, it is probable that a number of children assembled around him.

You have the sad story told in 1 Samuel 21:10-15. In after days, when David sang songs of praise to Jehovah, recollecting how he had become the laughing-stock of little children, he seemed to say, "Ah! by my folly before the children in the streets, I have lowered myself in the estimation of generations that shall live after me; now I will endeavor to undo the mischief—'Come, you children, hearken unto me—I will teach you the fear of the Lord.'" Very possibly, if David had never been in such a low position, he would never have thought of this duty; for I do not discover that he ever said in any other Psalm, "Come, you children, hearken unto me." He had the cares of his cities, his provinces, and his nation pressing upon him, and he may have been at other times but little attentive to the education of youth; but here, being brought into the lowest position which man could possibly occupy, having become as one bereft of reason, he recollects his duty. The exalted or prosperous Christian is not always mindful of "the lambs." That duty generally devolves on *Peters*, whose pride and confidence have been crushed, and who rejoice thus practically to answer their Lord's question, as the apostle did when Jesus said. to him, "Do you love Me?" "Come, you children, hearken unto me—I will teach you the fear of the Lord." The doctrine is, that **children are capable of being taught the fear of the Lord.**

Men are generally wisest—after they have been most foolish. David had been extremely foolish—and now he became truly wise; and being so, it was not likely that he would utter foolish sentiments, or give directions such as would be dictated by a weak mind. We have heard it said by some that children cannot understand the great mysteries of religion. We even know some Sunday-school teachers who cautiously avoid mentioning the great doctrines of the gospel, because they think the children are not able to receive them. Alas! the same mistake has crept into the pulpit; for it is currently believed, among a certain class of preachers, that many of the doctrines of the Word of God, although true, are not fit to be taught to the people, since they would pervert them to their own destruction. Away with such priestcraft! Whatever God has revealed—ought to be preached!

Whatever HE has revealed, if I am not capable of understanding it, I will still believe and preach it. I do hold that there is no doctrine of the Word of God which a child, if he is capable of salvation, is not capable of receiving. I would have children taught all the great doctrines of truth without a solitary exception, that they may in their after days hold fast by them.

I can bear witness that children can understand the Scriptures; for I am sure that, when but a child, I could have discussed many a knotty point of controversial theology, having heard both sides of the question freely stated among my father's circle of friends. In fact, children are capable of understanding some things in early life, which we hardly understand afterwards. Children have eminently a *simplicity of faith*, and simplicity of faith is akin to the highest knowledge; indeed, we know not that there is much distinction between the simplicity of a child—and the genius of the profoundest mind. He who receives things simply, as a child, will often have ideas which the man who is prone to make a syllogism of everything will never attain unto. If you wish to know whether children can be taught, I point you to many in our churches, and in pious families—not prodigies—but such as we frequently see—Timothys and Samuels, and little girls, too, who have early come to know a Savior's love. As soon as a child can sin, that child can, if God's grace assist it, believe and receive the Word of God. As soon as children can learn evil, be assured that they are competent, under the teaching of the Holy Spirit, to learn good.

Never go to your class with the thought that the children cannot comprehend you; for if you do not make them understand, it is possibly because you do not yourselves understand; if you do not teach children what you wish them to learn, it may be because *you are not fit* for the task; you should find out simpler words, more fitted for their capacity, and then you would discover that it was not the fault of the child—but the fault of the teacher, if he did not learn.

I hold that children are capable of salvation. He who, in Divine sovereignty, reclaimed the grey-haired sinner from the error of his ways, can turn a little child from his youthful follies. He who, in the eleventh hour, finds some standing idle in the market-place, and sends them into the vineyard, can and does call men at the dawning of the day to labor for Him. He who can change the course of a river when it has rolled onward, and become a mighty flood, can control a new-born rivulet leaping from its cradle-fountain, and make it run into the channel He desires. He can do all things—He can work upon children's hearts as He pleases, for all are under His control.

I will not stay to establish the doctrine, because I do not consider that any are so foolish as to doubt it. But, although you believe it, I fear many do not expect to hear of children being saved. Throughout the churches, I have noticed a kind of abhorrence of anything like child-piety. We are frightened at the idea of a little boy loving Christ; and if we hear of a little girl following the Savior, we say that *it is a youthful fancy, an early impression that will die away.* I beseech you, never treat child-piety with suspicion. It is a tender plant—do not brush it too hard.

I heard a tale, some time ago, which I believe to be perfectly authentic. A dear little girl, some five or six years old, a true lover of Jesus, requested of her mother that she might join the church. The mother told her she was too young, and the poor little thing was exceedingly grieved. After a while, the mother, who saw that piety was in her child's heart, spoke to the minister on the subject. The minister talked to the child, and said to the mother, "I am thoroughly convinced of her piety—but I cannot take her into the church, she is too young." When the child heard that, a strange gloom passed over her face; and the next morning, when the mother went to her little bed, she lay with a pearly tear on each eye, dead for very grief; her heart was broken, because she could not follow her Savior, and do as He had bidden her. I would not have murdered that child for a world! Take care how you treat young piety. Be very tender in dealing with it. Believe that children can be saved just as much as yourselves.

I do most firmly believe in the salvation of children. When you see the young heart brought to the Savior, do not stand by and speak harshly, mistrusting everything. It is better sometimes to be deceived—than to be the means of causing one of these little ones who believe in Jesus to stumble. May God send to His people a firm belief that little buds of grace are worthy of all tender care!

King David's two encouragements to parents and teachers

The first is that of **pious example**. David said, "Come, you children, hearken unto me—I will teach you the fear of the Lord." You are not ashamed to tread in the footsteps of David, are you? You will not object to follow the example of one who was first eminently holy, and then eminently great.

Shall the shepherd boy, the giant-slayer, the sweet psalmist of Israel, and the mighty monarch, leave footprints in which you are too proud to tread? Ah, no! you will be happy, I am sure, to be as David was. If you want, however, a higher example even than that of David, hear the Son of David while from His lips flow the sweet words, "Let the little children to come unto Me, and forbid them not, for of such is the Kingdom of Heaven." I am sure it would encourage you if you always thought of these examples. You who are teaching children, are not dishonored by that occupation. Some may say to you, "You are *only* a Sunday-school teacher," but you are a noble personage, holding an honorable office, and having illustrious predecessors.

We love to see people of some standing in society take an interest in Sunday-schools. One great fault in many of our churches is that the children are left for the *young people* to care for; the older members, who have more wisdom, taking but very little notice of them; and, very often, the wealthier members of the church stand aside as if the teaching of the poor were not (as indeed it is) the special business of the rich. I hope for the day when the mighty men of Israel shall be found helping in this great warfare against the enemy.

In the United States we have heard of Presidents, of Judges, Members of Congress, and people in the highest positions, not *condescending*, for I scorn to use such a term—but *honoring* themselves by teaching little children in Sunday-schools. He who teaches a class in a Sunday-school has earned a good degree. I had rather receive the title of S.S.T. than M.A., B.A., or any other honor that ever was conferred by men. Let me beg you, then, to take heart, because your duties are so honorable. Let the royal example of David, let the God-like example of Jesus Christ inspire you with fresh diligence and increasing ardor, with confident and enduring perseverance, still to go on in your blessed work, saying as David did, "Come, you children, hearken unto me—I will teach you the fear of the Lord!"

The second is the encouragement of **great success**. David said, "Come, you children, hearken unto me!" He did not add, "*perhaps* I will teach you the fear of the Lord," but, "I *will* teach you the fear of the Lord."

The success of Sunday-schools! If I begin to talk of that, I shall have an endless theme; therefore, I will not commence. Many volumes might be written on it, and then when all were written, we might say, "I suppose that even the world itself could not contain all that might be written." Up yonder, where the starry hosts perpetually sing God's high praises, up where the white-robed throng cast their crowns before His feet, we shall behold the success of Sunday-schools. And here, in almost every pulpit of our land, and there in the pews where the deacons sit, and godly members join in worship—there is seen the success of Sunday schools. And far away across yonder broad ocean, in the islets of the South, in lands where those dwell who bow before blocks of wood and stone, there are the missionaries who were saved in Sunday-schools, and the thousands, blessed by their labors, contribute to swell the mighty stream of the *incalculable*, I had almost said *infinite*, success of Sunday school instruction.

Go on with your holy service; much has been done already—but more shall yet be done. Let all your past victories inflame you with fresh ardor, let the remembrance of your triumphs in previous campaigns, and all trophies won for your Savior on the battle-field of the past, be your encouragement to press on with the duty of the present and the future!

CHILDHOOD AND HOLY SCRIPTURE

Paul taught young Timothy the gospel himself. Timothy not only *heard* his doctrine—but *saw* his practice. We cannot force truth upon men—but we can make our own *teaching* clear and decided, and make our *lives* consistent therewith. Truth and holiness are the surest antidotes to error and unrighteousness.

The apostle said to Timothy, "Continue in the things which you have learned and have been assured of—knowing of *whom* you have learned them." He then dwelt upon another potent remedy which had been of great service to the young preacher—namely, the knowing of the Holy Scriptures from his earliest childhood. This was to young Timothy one of his best safeguards. His early training held him like an anchor, and saved him from the dreadful drift of the age. Happy young man, of whom the apostle could say, "From a child you have known the Holy Scriptures, which are able to make you wise unto salvation through faith which is in Christ Jesus!"

To be prepared for the coming conflict, we have only to *preach* the gospel, and to *live* the gospel; and also to take care that we teach the children the Word of the Lord. This last is specially to be attended to, for it is by the mouth of babes and sucklings, that God will still the enemy. It is idle to dream that human learning must be met by human learning, or that Satan must cast out Satan. No! Lift up the *brazen serpent* wherever the fiery serpents are biting the people, and men shall look to it and live. Bring the children out, and turn their little eyes towards the divinely ordained remedy! There is still life in a look—life as against the varied venoms of the serpent which are now poisoning the blood of men. There is no cure after all for *midnight*—but the rising *sun*. And no hope remains for a dark world—but the light of the Gospel.

Shine forth, O Sun of Righteousness— and mist, and cloud, and darkness must disappear. Keep to the apostolic plans, and rest assured of apostolic success. Preach Christ; preach the Word in season and out of season—and teach the children. One of God's chief methods for preserving His fields from tares, is to sow them early with wheat.

The work of God's grace in Timothy commenced with early instructions, "*From a child* you have known the Holy Scriptures." Note the time for instruction. The expression, "from a child," might be better understood it we read it, "from a very child;" or, as the Revised Version has it, "from a babe." It does not mean a well-grown child, or youth—but a child just rising out of infancy. From a very child, Timothy had known the sacred writings. This expression is, no doubt, used to show that we cannot begin too early to imbue the minds of our children with Scriptural knowledge.

Babes receive impressions long before we are aware of the fact. During the first months of a child's life—it learns more than we imagine. It soon learns the love of its mother, and its own dependence; and if the mother is wise—it learns the meaning of *obedience,* and the necessity of yielding its will to the parent's will. This may be the *keynote* of its whole future life. If it learns *obedience* and *submission* early—it will save a thousand tears from the child's eyes, and as many

from the mother's heart! A special van-
tage-ground is lost—when even *baby-hood* is left uncultured.

The Holy Scriptures may be learned
by children as soon as they are capable
of understanding anything. It is a very
remarkable fact, which I have heard as-
serted by many teachers—that children
will learn to read out of the Bible better than from any other book. I scarcely
know why; it may, perhaps, be on account of the simplicity of the language;
but I believe it is so. A Biblical fact will
often be grasped when an incident of
common history is forgotten. There is
an adaptation in the Bible for human
beings of all ages, and therefore it has
a fitness for children. We make a mistake when we think that we must begin
with something else—and *lead up* to the
Scriptures.

The Bible is the book for the *peep of
day*. Parts of it are above a child's mind,
for they are above the comprehension
of the most advanced among us. There
are *depths* in it wherein *leviathan* may
swim; but there are also *brooks* in which
a *lamb* may wade. Wise teachers know
how to lead their little ones into the
green pastures beside the still waters.

I was noticing, in the life of that man
of God whose loss presses very heavily
upon many of our hearts—namely, the

Earl of Shaftesbury, that his first religious impressions were produced by a humble woman. The impressions which made him *"Shaftesbury, the man of God, and the friend of man"* were received in the nursery. He had a godly nurse who spoke to him of the things of God. He tells us that she died before he was seven years of age; clear proof that early in life his heart had been able to receive the seal of the Spirit of God, and to receive it by humble instrumentality. Blessed among women was she whose name we know not—but who wrought incalculable service for God and man by her holy teaching of the chosen child. Young mothers, note this.

Give us the first seven years of a child, with God's grace—and we may defy the world, the flesh, and the devil to ruin that immortal soul. Those first years, while yet the clay is soft and plastic, go far to decide the form of the vessel. Do not say that your office, you who teach the young—is in the least degree *inferior* to ours, whose main business is with older folks. No, you have the first of the children, and your impressions, as they come first, will endure last! Oh, that they may be godly, and only godly!

Among the thoughts that come to an old man before he enters Heaven, the most plentiful are those that aforetime visited him when he sat upon his mother's knee. That which made Dr. Guthrie ask for a child's hymn when he was dying—is but an instinct of our nature, which leads us to complete the circle by folding together the ends of life. Childlike things are dearest to old age. The old songs are on our lips, and the old thoughts are in our minds. The teachings of our childhood leave clean-cut and sharp impressions upon the mind, which remain after seventy years have passed. Let us see that such *early impressions* are made for the highest ends.

It is well to note the admirable selection of **instructors**. We are not at a loss to tell **who** instructed youthful Timothy. In the first chapter of this epistle Paul says, "When I call to remembrance the sincere faith that is in you, which dwelt first in your **grandmother** Lois, and your **mother** Eunice; and I am persuaded that in you also." No doubt grandmother Lois and mother Eunice united in teaching the little one. Who should teach the children—but the parents? Timothy's father was a Greek, and probably a heathen—but his child was happy in having a venerable grandmother, so often the dearest of all relatives to a little child. He had also a gracious mother, once a devout Jewess—and afterwards also a firmly believing Christian, who made it her daily pleasure to teach her own dear child the Word of the Lord.

O dear mothers, you have a very sacred trust reposed in you by God! He has in effect said to you, "Take this child and nurse it for Me, and I will give you your wages!" You are called to equip the future man of God, that he may be thoroughly furnished unto every good work. If God spares you, you may live to hear that pretty boy speak the gospel to thousands, and you will have the sweet reflection in your heart that *the quiet teachings of the nursery* led the man to love God and serve Him.

Those who think that a mother detained at home by her little family is doing nothing, think the *reverse* of what is true. Scarcely may the godly mother be able to leave her home for a place of worship; but do not dream that she is lost to the work of the church; far from it, she is doing the best possible service for her Lord! Mothers, the godly training of your offspring is your first and most pressing duty. Christian women, by teaching children the Holy Scriptures, are as much fulfilling their part for the Lord, as Moses in judging Israel, or Solomon in building the temple!

Parents! Your children are as surely as grown-up people, "**dead** in trespasses and sins!" May no parent fail fully to realize the spiritual state in which **all** human beings are naturally found. Unless you have a very clear sense of **the utter ruin and spiritual death of your children**, you will be incapable of being made a blessing to them. Go to them, I beg you, not as to 'sleepers' whom you can by your own power awaken from their slumber— but as to 'spiritual corpses' who can only be quickened by a divine power!

If you think that your child is 'not really depraved', if you indulge foolish notions about the 'innocence of childhood', it should not surprise you if you remain barren and unfruitful.

If you would bring spiritual life to your child—you must most vividly realize that child's state. It is dead, dead! God will have you feel that your child is dead in trespasses and sins—as you once were. God would have you come into contact with that death by painful, crushing, humbling sympathy. If you would raise **your dead child** to spiritual life—you must feel the chill and horror of *your child's death* yourself. You must have, more or less, a distinct sense of the dreadful wrath of God, and of the terrors of the judgment to come. Depend upon it, when the spiritual death of your children alarms and overwhelms you—then it is that God is about to bless you!

CPSIA information can be obtained
at www.ICGtesting.com
Printed in the USA
LVHW050332300123
738202LV00013B/627